The Plastic-free Challenge

Written by Joshua Hatch

Illustrated by Ian Forss

Flying Start
to Literacy®

Contents

Chapter 1

The announcement

Every night, dinner at my house is the same. I set the table. My younger brother, Hugo, feeds the cat. Dad serves us whatever food he has made. Mum starts asking questions.

But this night was different.

"I have an announcement to make," said Mum.

This was a bad sign. Usually, when Mum makes an "announcement", it means bad news for Hugo and me.

Like the time she announced that Sundays would be screen-free days. Or the time she announced that Tuesdays and Thursdays would be sugar-free days!

We braced ourselves for today's announcement.

"Did you know that a family like ours – mum, dad, two kids – throws away almost 450 kilograms of plastic a year? And almost all of it ends up in the ocean."

"That's terrible!" my dad said.

"It is," said Mum. "So let's do something to help. Let's go plastic-free."

I looked at Hugo and rolled my eyes. I expected he would do the same. Instead, he eagerly joined in.

"Today in summer camp, we watched a program about the Great Pacific Garbage Patch in the ocean."

"Oh?" said Mum, her eyebrows raised.

"Millions of pieces of tiny plastic garbage have ended up in the Pacific Ocean," he explained. "Fish eat it and get sick. It's horrible. Going plastic-free seems like a great idea."

My brother is the worst!

I was annoyed. Why did we always have to be different? Why couldn't we be like other families?

"I think it's a *stu*–," I started to say.

My dad shot me a look that made it clear I shouldn't say what I was about to say.

"I mean, how is that even possible?" I said. "Plastic is everywhere."

Chapter 2
Going plastic-free

The challenge of living without plastic became clear pretty quickly. The day after the announcement, I asked Dad to take me back-to-school shopping.

"Sure thing," he said. "Grab your list and let's go."

"Can I come, too?" asked Hugo.

Before I could say no, Hugo had jumped in the car.

* * * * *

As I walked down the aisle at the shop, I grabbed a packet of mechanical pencils, some ballpoint pens, a shiny pink pencil case and a cute purple binder.

"Hmm . . . plastic, plastic and plastic," said Dad. "Let's see if we can find some alternatives."

"I can!" said Hugo excitedly.

There's a reason little brothers are known for being annoying.

In a flash, he returned with some wooden pencils, a metal pen, a wooden pencil box and a binder made of recycled cardboard.

I could feel my face turning red and I wanted to scream.

"A *cardboard binder*?" I asked, with an attitude that made it clear I was not pleased.

"What's the problem with cardboard?" Dad asked.

"It looks ugly," I said, holding back tears. What would my friends think?

"I think it's pretty cool," said Hugo.

"Me, too," added Dad. "You could draw on it."

"Fine," I said. But it was not fine. They just didn't get it – I was going to be the laughing stock of my school.

* * * * *

Back at home, Mum was unpacking groceries, but they weren't our normal groceries. She had glass jars of nuts and honey, and milk and juice in paper cartons!

"And I have a surprise for both of you," she said. "New lunch boxes!"

Oh no! Hugo was delighted with his, but mine was the ugliest-looking lunch box I had ever seen. It was made from metal and it was a monster. I decided I needed to speak out.

"This whole no-plastic thing is getting out of hand," I said.

"What makes you say that?" said Mum.

"I just want to live a normal life," I said. "I have plain and boring school supplies, and now I have a super-ugly lunch box. It's a real pain."

"Speaking of things that are a pain,"
my dad piped up. "The rubbish needs to
go out." He looked at me.

As I pulled the paper rubbish bag out of
the bin, garbage juice leaked all over my
new canvas shoes.

"Ah!" I screamed. "This is disgusting!
And so stupid!"

I threw the bag down on the kitchen floor,
ran to my room and slammed the door.

After a couple of minutes, my dad knocked on the door and came into my room. I knew I would be in trouble for shouting and leaving rubbish all over the floor. I expected him to be pretty mad.

"Hey, kiddo," he said in a soft voice that I wasn't expecting. "I understand you're frustrated. Maybe you're thinking, 'Why can't we just be like everyone else?'"

It was exactly what I was thinking, but I didn't admit to it.

"Here's the thing. If we just do what everyone else does, nothing will ever change. Nothing will get better. Change is hard. Doing the right thing is hard."

I listened but didn't respond.

"And every little bit matters," he added.
"Imagine you're a sea turtle. You get a
piece of plastic stuck in your nostril. You
have no way to get it out. It's just one
piece of plastic, but for that turtle, it
matters a lot."

Then Dad kissed my forehead and left the room.

Chapter 3
Back to school

On the first day back at school, I was nervous. Would my friends notice my plastic-free stuff?

At the school gates, I saw my friends Lucia and Kevin.

"Are you excited for school?" Lucia asked.

Excited isn't the word I would have picked, but I nodded.

"I can't wait to see Mr Robbins," Lucia said, referring to our gym teacher. "He's so funny!"

In class, Lucia nudged me. "Can I borrow a pen?"

I opened my backpack and pulled out my new wooden pencil box.

"Oh, what is that?" Lucia said.

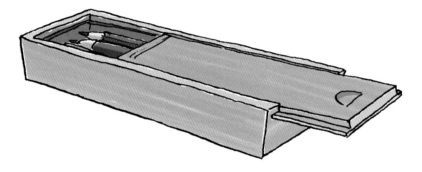

"It's a pencil box. My dad bought it for me." I quickly opened it to get a pen and then put the box back in my bag.

"Whoa!" she exclaimed. "What's with the fancy-pants pen?"

"Oh, it's a long story," I whispered. "I'll explain later."

* * * * *

At lunch, I found a seat near the doors that led outside. I wanted to sit as close to freedom as I could.

"What's that?" asked Lucia, when she saw my lunch box.

"Um," I stammered as I tried to hide it.

"How come you have all this new fancy stuff that's so different?" she asked.

"My parents," I said. "They've banned plastic from our house."

"Why are they doing that?" Lucia asked. "Did they hit their heads?" She giggled and then I did, too.

"They think using less plastic will be better for the environment," I said, rolling my eyes.

I set my food out on the table. My sandwich was wrapped in paper instead of tucked inside a plastic bag.

Just then, Kevin came over. "What is that?" he said, pointing at my lunch box.

"Nothing," I said as I quickly hid it in my backpack.

"Hey, let me see it," said Kevin.

Luckily, Lucia distracted him by singing her new favourite song. Kevin joined in.

Me? It was my favourite song, too, but I couldn't join in. I just sat there with my paper-wrapped sandwich, hiding my metal monster lunch box, and feeling like I would never fit in!

* * * * *

That night at dinner, Mum asked how my day was.

"Terrible," I said.

"Why?" she asked.

"Because you and Dad and Hugo are ruining my life!"

I threw down my knife and fork, and ran to my room. I slammed the door and flopped down on the bed, crying.

Chapter 4
Plastic-free cool!

The next morning, my metal monster lunch box sat on the counter. As I headed out the door, I "forgot" it.

"Hey there, kiddo!" Dad called out. "Don't forget your lunch box." I trudged back into the house.

"You okay?" asked Dad. "What's wrong?"

"Yesterday, everyone noticed my new stuff, but not in a good way," I said.

"Are you sure?" asked Dad.

I nodded, but the more I thought about it, the less sure I was.

* * * * *

As I got settled in homeroom, Lucia came up to me.

"I want to give this back to you," she said, handing me my metal pen. "And I want to show you this."

Lucia had a pen, just like the one I had given her.

"It's really nice. Instead of throwing it out when it's out of ink, I can just refill it with more ink. Better for the environment!"

I smiled and Lucia smiled back.

At lunchtime, I kept my lunch box under the table and set my food on the table. Lucia sat down next to me. Then I saw Kevin headed our way.

"What's for lunch?" I asked.

"Oh, I have a surprise," he said.

Uh–oh, I thought. My heart sank.

"When I saw your lunch box yesterday," he said, "I liked it so much, I made my mum take me to the shops so I could get one like it."

"Really?" I asked.

"Well, almost like it," Kevin answered. "I got one with a picture of my favourite band on it!"

I looked down and my face turned bright red. But Kevin wasn't making fun of me.

"What's wrong?" asked Kevin. I could tell he was confused.

"I'm sorry, I thought you were making fun of me."

"Why would I do that?" said Kevin.

"Because my parents are always coming up with goofy ideas. They say plastic is bad for the environment, and so we shouldn't use it. That's why I have this metal monster."

"Oh!" Kevin exclaimed. "My parents have been trying to make us use less plastic, too."

"Really?" I said.

"Yeah. It's not banned at our house, but we're trying to use less. Your lunch box is cool – really cool."

"I want one, too," said Lucia.

This time, when Lucia and Kevin started singing our favourite song, I joined in, too.

At dinner that night, my mum asked the question she always asks.

"How was school?"

"Great," I said. Dad looked at me, surprised.

"You were right, Dad. Turns out Kevin and Lucia were impressed. Lucia bought a pen like mine and Kevin got a metal lunch box. His family is trying to use less plastic, too."

"Oh," said Mum. "So maybe this 'plastic-free' idea isn't so bad after all?"

Everyone laughed.

Then Hugo said, "You know, next we should try to stop using electricity."

Before Mum could reply, I jumped in.

"Don't even think about it!"

A note from the author

I keep reading news stories about wildlife being injured by plastic: whales with plastic in their stomachs, birds with plastic wrapped around their beaks and turtles with plastic straws stuck in them. This breaks my heart. They don't deserve that. And we can do better.

Do we really need to use so much plastic? In writing this book, I realised we make choices every day. Maybe we could choose to return to more traditional, reusable materials. Now when I go grocery shopping, I look for glass or metal containers. I avoid plastic bags. Instead, I use reusable cloth bags.

I hope you'll consider doing the same. Then we would really make a difference.